UNDERGROUND HABITATS

Molly Aloian and Bobbie Kalman

🌱 Crabtree Publishing Company

www.crabtreebooks.com

Introducing Habitats

Created by Bobbie Kalman

Dedicated by Molly Aloian
For Allison and Connor Watson, two of the brightest children I know!

FSC
Mixed Sources
Cert no. SW-COC-001271
© 1996 FSC

Editor-in-Chief
Bobbie Kalman

Writing team
Molly Aloian
Bobbie Kalman

Substantive editor
Kathryn Smithyman

Editors
Michael Hodge
Kelley MacAulay

Design
Margaret Amy Salter
Samantha Crabtree
(cover and series logo)

Production coordinator
Heather Fitzpatrick

Photo research
Crystal Foxton

Special thanks to
Jack Pickett and Karen Van Atte

Illustrations
Barbara Bedell: pages 14, 32 (top and bottom right)
Katherine Kantor: page 20
Bonna Rouse: pages 6, 10
Margaret Amy Salter: pages 13, 15, 32 (bottom left)

Photographs
Animals Animals - Earth Scenes: © Dragesco-Joffe, Alain: page 24;
    © Pryor, Maresa: page 29; © Schwartz, C.W.: page 27;
    © Whitehead, Fred: page 25; © Wilkinson, Ernest: page 30
Bruce Coleman Inc.: Gary Zahm: page 22
iStockphoto.com: Loic Bernard: page 6; Bruce MacQueen: page 4
Bobbie Kalman: page 15 (middle left)
© Mike Potts/naturepl.com: page 26
Photo Researchers, Inc.: Jacana: page 28; Tom McHugh: page 9;
    Anthony Mercieca: page 19 (top); Rod Planck: pages 7, 8
© ShutterStock.com/Jackie Foster: page 3
Visuals Unlimited: Joe McDonald: page 19 (bottom); Jim Merli: page 31;
    M.J. O'Riain & J. Jarvis: page 17; Michael Redmer: page 14
© Rich Wagner/WildNaturePhotos: page 16
Other images by Corbis, Corel, Digital Stock, Digital Vision,
    Otto Rogge Photography, Photodisc, and TongRo Image Stock

Library and Archives Canada Cataloguing in Publication

Aloian, Molly
    Underground habitats / Molly Aloian & Bobbie Kalman.

(Introducing habitats)
ISBN-13: 978-0-7787-2954-9 (bound)
ISBN-13: 978-0-7787-2982-2 (pbk.)
ISBN-10: 0-7787-2954-0 (bound)
ISBN-10: 0-7787-2982-6 (pbk.)

    1. Underground ecology--Juvenile literature. 2. Burrowing
animals--Juvenile literature. I. Kalman, Bobbie, date. II. Title.
III. Series.

QL756.15.A46 2006   j577   C2006-904509-7

Library of Congress Cataloging-in-Publication Data

Aloian, Molly.
    Underground habitats / Molly Aloian & Bobbie Kalman.
      p. cm. -- (Introducing habitats)
    ISBN-13: 978-0-7787-2954-9 (rlb)
    ISBN-10: 0-7787-2954-0 (rlb)
    ISBN-13: 978-0-7787-2982-2 (pb)
    ISBN-10: 0-7787-2982-6 (pb)
    1. Burrowing animals--Juvenile literature. 2. Underground ecology--
Juvenile literature. I. Kalman, Bobbie. II. Title. III. Series.

QL756.15.A46 2007
591.56'48--dc22

2006024904

Crabtree Publishing Company

www.crabtreebooks.com   1-800-387-7650

Copyright © **2007 CRABTREE PUBLISHING COMPANY**. All rights reserved. No part of this publication may be reproduced, stored in a retrieval system or be transmitted in any form or by any means, electronic, mechanical, photocopying, recording, or otherwise, without the prior written permission of Crabtree Publishing Company. In Canada: We acknowledge the financial support of the Government of Canada through the Book Publishing Industry Development Program (BPIDP) for our publishing activities.

Published in Canada
Crabtree Publishing
616 Welland Ave.
St. Catharines, ON
L2M 5V6

Published in the United States
Crabtree Publishing
PMB16A
350 Fifth Ave., Suite 3308
New York, NY 10118

Published in the United Kingdom
Crabtree Publishing
White Cross Mills
High Town, Lancaster
LA1 4XS

Published in Australia
Crabtree Publishing
386 Mt. Alexander Rd.
Ascot Vale (Melbourne)
VIC 3032

Contents

What is a habitat?

A **habitat** is a place in nature.
Plants live in habitats. Animals
live in habitats, too. Some animals
make homes in their habitats.

Living and non-living things

There are **living things** in habitats. Plants and animals are living things. There are also **non-living things** in habitats. Rocks, water, and dirt are non-living things.

Everything they need

Plants and animals need air, water, and food to stay alive. Plants and animals have everything they need in their habitats. This marmot found a plant to eat in its habitat.

At home in their habitats

Some animals make homes in their habitats. This desert cottontail rabbit made a home in its habitat. Its home is inside a hole. The hole goes under the ground.

Dirty and dark

Some animals live in underground habitats. Underground habitats are dirty places! They are filled with soil, rocks, and sand. This star-nosed mole lives in an underground habitat. Bits of dirt and sand stick to underground animals.

Lights out!

Underground habitats are dark. They are dark because the sun does not shine under the ground. This kangaroo rat lives in a dark underground habitat. It has big eyes. Having big eyes helps the kangaroo rat see in the dark.

Roots in soil

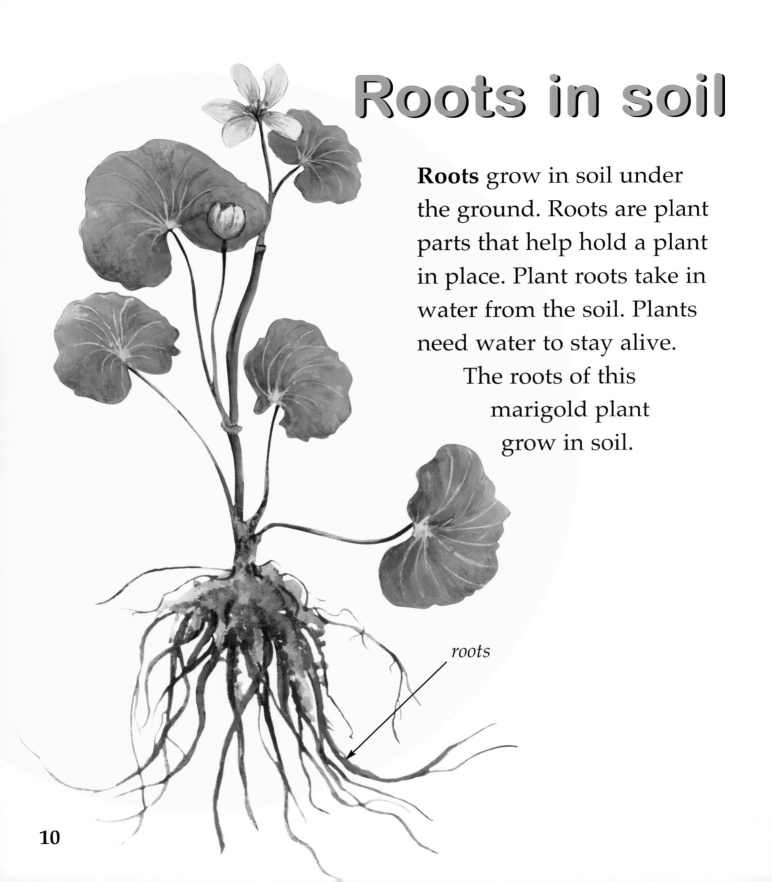

Roots grow in soil under the ground. Roots are plant parts that help hold a plant in place. Plant roots take in water from the soil. Plants need water to stay alive. The roots of this marigold plant grow in soil.

roots

Leaves above the ground

These small plants have tiny roots.
The roots grow under the ground. The
plants also have stems and small leaves.
The stems and leaves grow above the
ground. The roots, stems, and leaves
will grow bigger as the plants grow.

leaf

stem

Making food

Living things need food to stay alive. Plants make their own food. They make food from sunlight, air, and water. Making food from sunlight, air, and water is called **photosynthesis**.

Plant food

A plant gets sunlight through its leaves. It also gets air through its leaves. A plant gets water through its roots. A plant uses sunlight, air, and water to make food.

Leaves take in air.

Leaves take in sunlight.

Roots take in water from soil.

Underground animals

Many animals live in underground habitats. The animals on these pages live in underground habitats. Their bodies are suited to living under the ground.

A rabbit has strong legs. It uses its legs to dig a home under the ground.

A great plains toad uses its two back feet to dig into sand or dirt.

An earthworm finds tiny plants and animals to eat under the ground.

Ants live under the ground to stay hidden from animals that eat them.

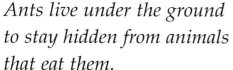

Yellow jackets live in underground homes called **nests**. They make their nests out of plant parts.

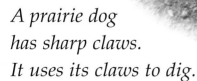

A prairie dog has sharp claws. It uses its claws to dig.

When a meerkat becomes too hot, it goes under the ground to cool off.

15

Dig it!

Many animals that live under the ground are good at digging. They have strong legs and feet. They use their legs and feet to dig through dirt and sand. This spadefoot toad is using its back legs and feet to dig into the ground.

Teeth for digging

Some animals that live under the ground
have strong, long teeth. They use their
teeth to dig through dirt. This naked
mole rat is using its teeth to dig. The
mole rat's lips close behind its teeth.
Its lips close behind its teeth so the
animal will not get dirt in its mouth.

Finding food

Animals must eat food to stay alive. Some animals find food under the ground. Others find food above the ground. Some animals eat plants. Animals that eat plants are called **herbivores**. This desert tortoise is a herbivore. It eats leaves, bark, and grass.

Eating animals

Some animals are **carnivores**.
Carnivores are animals
that eat other animals.
This burrowing owl
is a carnivore.
It caught a
mouse to eat.

Eating anyting

Some animals are
omnivores. Omnivores
eat both plants and
animals. This nine-
banded armadillo is
an omnivore. It eats
fruit and insects.

19

Getting energy

All living things need **energy**. They need energy to grow and to move. Energy comes from the sun. Plants get energy from the sun. Animals cannot get energy from the sun. They get energy by eating other living things. A prairie dog is a herbivore. It gets energy by eating grass.

sun

grass

prairie dog

Eating animals

Carnivores get energy by eating other animals. This badger is a carnivore. It gets energy by eating a prairie dog.

badger

Underground homes

Different underground animals make different underground homes. Many animals dig holes or tunnels called **burrows**. This crayfish lives in a burrow. Other animals dig holes called **dens**. Badgers make underground homes called **setts**. Rabbit homes are called **warrens**.

Part of a group

Some animals live alone in their underground homes. Other animals live in groups. This meerkat group lives in a burrow.

23

Keeping cool

Some animals live in parts of the world
that have hot weather. Many of these
animals live under the ground. They
live under the ground to keep cool.
This desert jerboa lives in a hot desert.
It is digging an underground home.
It will stay cool in its home.

Cool nights

In some parts of the world, the weather is very hot during the day. The weather is cooler at night. Some animals stay under the ground during the day. They go above the ground at night when the weather is cooler. This nine-banded armadillo is crawling out of its home. It goes above the ground at night.

Staying warm

The weather gets very cold in some parts of the world. Cold winds blow. Snow falls on the ground. Some animals make tunnels under the snow. The animals stay warm inside the tunnels. This lemming is coming out of its warm tunnel to look for food.

Going under

Winter weather is too cold for this box turtle. Before winter begins, the turtle digs a burrow under the ground. It goes to sleep inside its burrow. Sleeping under the ground keeps the box turtle warm. When the weather gets warm in spring, the box turtle wakes up. It goes above the ground again.

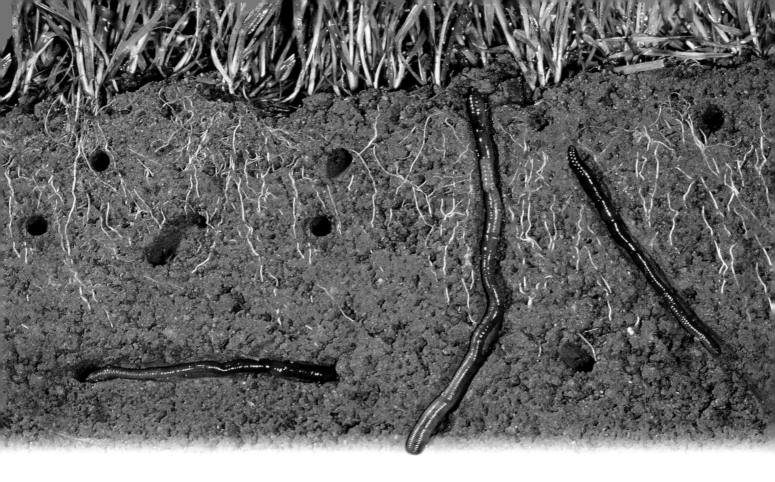

Staying safe

Animals in underground habitats are
safe from the animals that want to eat them.
Underground animals are safe because they
are hidden in dirt. These earthworms are
safe because they are hidden in dirt.

Safe places

Underground animals sometimes go above the ground. When other animals get too close, underground animals leap back into their underground homes. This kangaroo rat is leaping into its burrow.

Having babies

Some underground animals have babies in their homes. The babies are safe in their underground homes. This mother badger and her babies are inside their burrow. Baby badgers are called **cubs**.

Down below

This mother pine snake made a burrow under the ground. She laid eggs in the burrow. Some animals eat snake eggs. The animals may not be able to find the eggs in the burrow. Baby snakes will hatch from the eggs.

Words to know and Index

animals
pages 4, 5, 6, 8,
14-15, 16, 17, 18, 19,
20, 21, 22, 23, 24, 25,
26, 28, 29, 30, 31

burrows
pages 22, 23, 27,
29, 30, 31

digging
pages 14, 15, 16, 17,
22, 24

energy
pages 20, 21

food
pages 6, 12, 13,
18, 26

habitats
pages 4, 5, 6, 7, 8, 9,
14, 28

homes
pages 4, 7, 14, 15,
22, 23, 24, 29, 30

plants
pages 4, 5, 6, 10,
11, 12, 13, 14, 15,
18, 19, 20

Other index words
bodies 14
carnivores 19, 21
herbivores 18, 20
living things 5, 12, 20
non-living things 5
omnivores 19
photosynthesis 12

Printed in Canada — FR